D0847175

WHAT IS AN
INSECT?

Robert Snedden

Photographs by Oxford Scientific Films

Illustrated by Adrian Lascom

Sierra Club Books for Children

San Francisco

The Sierra Club, founded in 1892 by John Muir, has devoted itself to the study and protection of the earth's scenic and ecological resources—mountains, wetlands, woodlands, wild shores and rivers, deserts and plains. The publishing program of the Sierra Club offers books to the public as a nonprofit educational service in the hope that they may enlarge the public's understanding of the Club's basic concerns. The Sierra Club has some sixty chapters in the United States and in Canada. For information about how you may participate in its programs to preserve wilderness and the quality of life, please address inquiries to Sierra Club, 730 Polk Street, San Francisco, CA 94109.

Text copyright © 1992 by Robert Snedden
Photographs copyright © 1992 by Oxford Scientific Films and individual copyright holders
Format and illustrations copyright © 1992 by Belitha Press Limited

All rights reserved under International and Pan-American Copyright Conventions. No part of this book may be reproduced in any form or by any electronic or mechanical means, including information storage and retrieval systems, without permission in writing from the publisher.

First U.S. Edition 1993

First published in Great Britain in 1992 by Belitha Press Limited, 31 Newington Green, London N16 9PU

Library of Congress Cataloging-in-Publication data is available from Sierra Club Books for Children, 100 Bush Street, 13th Floor, San Francisco, CA 94104

Printed in China for Imago

10 9 8 7 6 5 4 3 2 1

Editor: Rachel Cooke
Designer: Frances McKay
Consultant: Dr. Jim Flegg
Educational consultant: Brenda Hart

The publisher wishes to thank the following for permission to reproduce copyrighted material:

Oxford Scientific Films and individual copyright holders on the following pages: G. I. Bernard, 5 bottom, 10 left, 11 top left, 21 right; Mike Birkhead, title page; Neil Bromhall, 11 bottom left; George K. Bryce/Animals Animals, 14 top; J. A. L. Cooke, 10 bottom, 14/15; John Cooke, 15 top; Michael Fogden, 16/17, 27 left; D. G. Fox, contents page, 4 bottom; Harry Fox, 26; Bob Fredrick, 9 top; Breck P. Kent/Animals Animals, 22/23; London Scientific Films, 19 bottom; Alastair MacEwen, 19 top; G. A. Maclean, cover, 5 top; Colin Milkins, 12; Patti Murray/Animals Animals, 18, 20/21; Stan Osolinski, 21 left; Oxford Scientific Films, 23 top; Helen W. Price, 22 top; Avril Ramage, 10 top; Kjell Sandved, 20 bottom; Dr. Friedrich Sauer/Okapia, 27 top; David Shale, 11 right; D. R. Specker/Animals Animals, 16 left; Sinclair Stammers, 28/29; Harold Taylor, 17 top; K. G. Vock/Okapia, 4 top; P. & W. Ward, 27 bottom.

THE SCARBOROUGH PUBLIC LIBRARY BOARD

Front cover picture:
A peacock butterfly.

Title page picture:
A garden tiger moth sucks sugary nectar from a flower.

Contents page picture:
The caterpillar of a death's-head hawk moth.

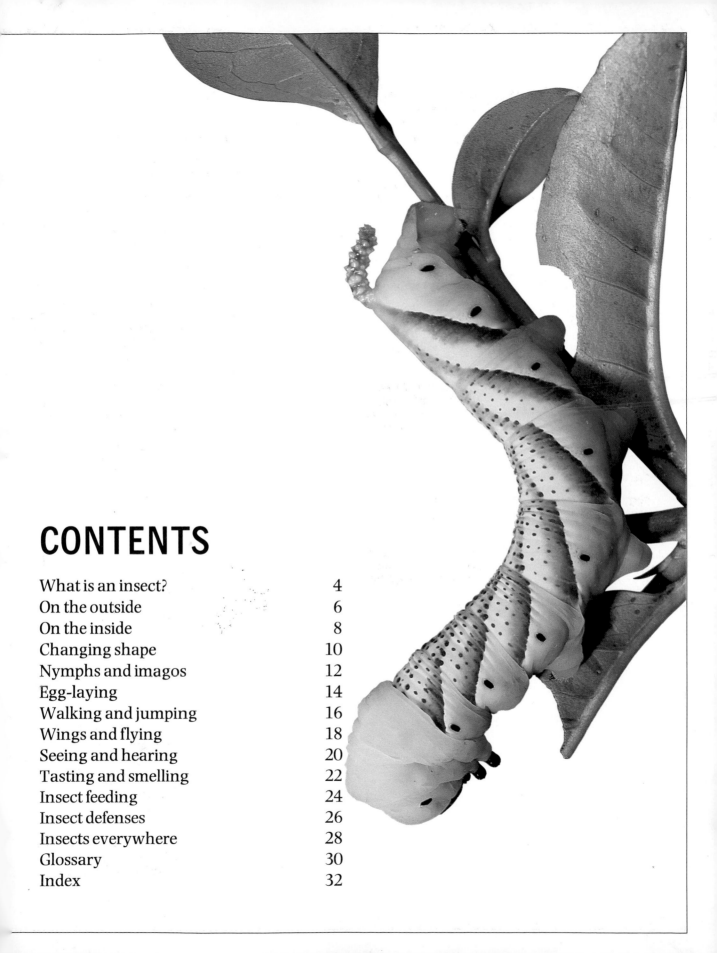

CONTENTS

What is an insect?	4
On the outside	6
On the inside	8
Changing shape	10
Nymphs and imagos	12
Egg-laying	14
Walking and jumping	16
Wings and flying	18
Seeing and hearing	20
Tasting and smelling	22
Insect feeding	24
Insect defenses	26
Insects everywhere	28
Glossary	30
Index	32

WHAT IS AN INSECT?

What do you think an insect is? Perhaps you think it is a very small animal with lots of legs. Well, that is close, but how *many* legs does it have? Six? Eight? Or more?

Maybe you think that insects are very small animals with lots of legs that can fly. That is a better way of describing an insect because all of the very small, many-legged *flying* animals that you see *are* insects.

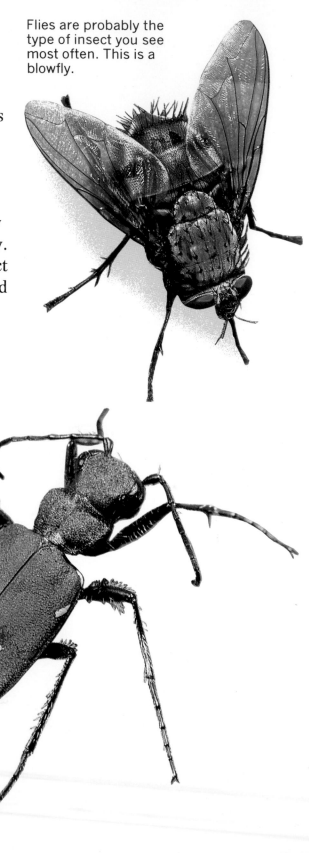

Flies are probably the type of insect you see most often. This is a blowfly.

A beetle has two pairs of wings. One pair forms a hard case to protect the other. This is a green tiger beetle.

4

Butterflies often have beautiful, multi-colored wings. This is a peacock butterfly.

This is a thrip, a tiny insect that lives in plants. You can see its narrow wings folded over its back.

But do all insects fly? And do all insects have lots of legs? Sometimes knowing whether or not an animal is an insect can be tricky. What about animals that might be insects but don't fly? What about ants and spiders? Are they both insects? Are caterpillars insects?

Insects come in many shapes and forms, from butterflies to beetles and from thrips to flies. This book should help you to decide just what *is* an insect and also what *is not*.

ON THE OUTSIDE

One way of telling whether or not an animal is an insect is to look at its body. A fully grown **adult** insect is divided into three parts. These parts are called the **head**, the **thorax** and the **abdomen**. The insects, in their adult form, are the only animals that are divided up in this way.

The head is where the insect's mouth parts, eyes and **antennae** are found. Almost all insects have a pair of antennae, or feelers, on their heads. Most types of insect have more than two eyes – two large eyes and usually three smaller, simpler ones.

The thorax is the middle part of an insect's body. It is where the insect's legs and wings are attached. It is divided into three sections. Each section has a pair of legs attached. All adult insects have six legs. They never have more than six, so this is one way you can tell whether or not an animal is an insect. Spiders, for instance, always have eight legs, so they are *not* insects. Almost all types of insect have either one or two pairs of wings. These are also attached to the thorax.

The end part of the insect is called its abdomen. Many types of insect have another pair of feelers at the end of their abdomens.

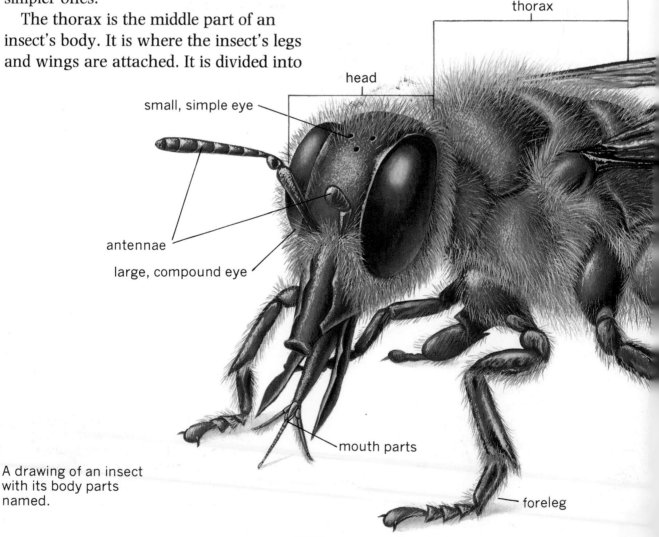

thorax

head

small, simple eye

antennae

large, compound eye

mouth parts

foreleg

A drawing of an insect with its body parts named.

An insect does not have bones inside its body like you do. Instead, the whole of its body and legs are covered by a hard skin, or **cuticle**, made of a material called **chitin**. This strengthens and supports the body, doing the same job as the **skeleton** inside you. This chitin coat is called an **exoskeleton**, which means "outside skeleton." Other animals, such as crabs, lobsters, spiders and centipedes, also have an exoskeleton.

▲ It is difficult to see that the bodies of some insects, such as these shield bugs, are divided into three parts, because their wings cover both the abdomen and thorax.

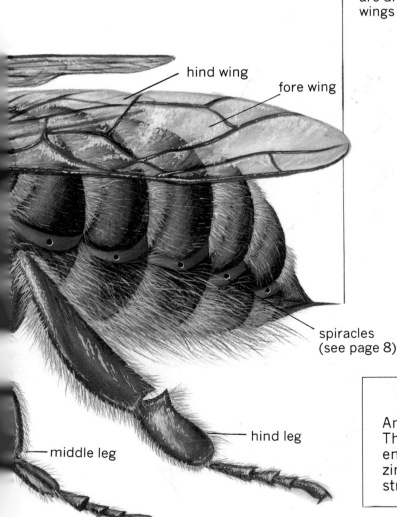

abdomen

hind wing

fore wing

spiracles
(see page 8)

hind leg

middle leg

Did you know?

An insect's outer coat is very tough. The jaws of some beetles are strong enough to bite through copper and zinc metal, so their jaws must be stronger than the metal.

ON THE INSIDE

An insect's body is very different from yours. For instance, insects don't take air in through their mouths but through small holes in the sides of their thorax and abdomen. These holes are called **spiracles**. The spiracles lead into a system of air tubes that branch out into the insect's body, getting smaller and smaller. These are called **trachea**.

Insects don't have **veins** and **arteries** to carry their blood around their bodies like you do. The blood simply surrounds the parts inside their bodies. An insect's heart is a long tube that runs along its back. It keeps the insect's blood moving around its body. Insect blood is usually green.

Running through the middle of an insect's body is its **digestive system**. This is where it takes the nourishment from its food. Some types of insects have a muscular part in the digestive system called a **gizzard**. This helps them to grind up tough or hard food. Many types of bird have gizzards too.

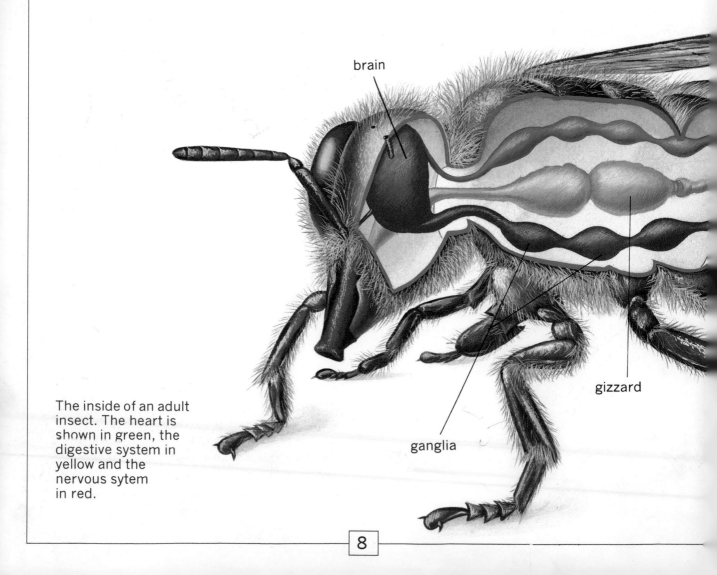

brain

gizzard

ganglia

The inside of an adult insect. The heart is shown in green, the digestive system in yellow and the nervous sytem in red.

The **nervous system** carries messages from one part of the body to another. When you want to move your arm, your brain sends a message to your arm to make it move. An insect's nervous system is fairly simple compared to yours. Instead of its brain doing most of the control work, it also has parts called **ganglia**. Each of these is responsible for controlling a different part of the insect's body. For instance, there is a ganglion in the head that controls feeding and ganglia in the thorax that control flying and walking.

This caterpillar's spiracles can be clearly seen. They are the black spots along its middle. Find out more about caterpillars on page 10.

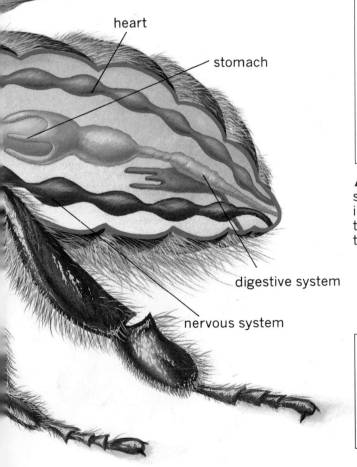

heart

stomach

digestive system

nervous system

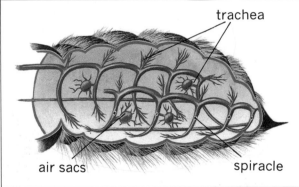

trachea

air sacs

spiracle

▲ This diagram shows the spiracles on the side of an insect's abdomen and the internal network of air tubes and trachea that they lead to. This network extends throughout the insect's body.

Did you know?

An insect's blood carries digested food around its body. It doesn't carry oxygen like the blood of birds and larger animals.

CHANGING SHAPE

All insects hatch from eggs, some while still inside the parent. Eggs are produced by the adult female insect, usually in large numbers.

Most insects hatch from their eggs looking completely unlike the way they will look as adults. For example, caterpillars don't look at all like the butterflies or moths they will become.

▲ These black and yellow caterpillars will turn into moths with bright red spots and stripes.

At this stage of its life the insect is called a **larva**. The word for more than one larva is larvae. Maggots are the larvae of flies. Wasp and bee larvae are called grubs.

The larvae of different insects have different forms. Fly maggots have no legs. They don't need to get around much because they usually hatch out surrounded by food. The grubs of bees and wasps don't need legs either. They are looked after by adult insects in the nest.

Life cycle of a ladybird

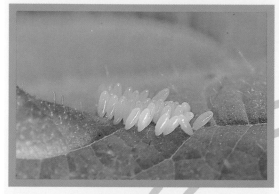

1 These ladybird eggs have been laid on a nettle leaf. The larvae that hatch from them will find plenty to eat here.

An adult ladybird. The adults hunt and eat aphids just like the larvae do.

4

This ladybird larva has caught an aphid to eat. Aphids are tiny insects that are found in large numbers on many plants in summer.

2

The larvae of many beetles are active hunters and have legs to get around with. For instance, ladybird larvae look for other insects such as aphids to eat.

The change from a larva into an adult insect is one of the most remarkable things in all of nature. When it is fully grown the larva stops moving and grows a tough skin. During this stage it is called a **pupa**.

▲ Like the grubs of bees and wasps, the white, legless hornet grubs are well protected inside the nest. The adult hornets bring them food.

Many types of pupa are protected inside a **cocoon** that the larva makes for itself. Other types may be found under the ground or inside plants.

Hidden inside the pupa, the insect's body changes from a larva into an adult. This change is called **metamorphosis**. When the change is complete the pupa splits open and the adult insect crawls out.

Protected inside this pupa case, a ladybird larva will turn into an adult insect.

3

NYMPHS AND IMAGOS

Some young insects hatch from their eggs looking almost exactly like the adults they will grow into. The young of grasshoppers and earwigs are like this, for example. Young insects that look very much like their parents are called **nymphs**. The main difference is that only adults have wings.

As the nymph grows, every so often it has to shed its skin. It must do this because its hard cuticle case cannot grow and can only stretch a little. This shedding of the skin is called molting. The insect may molt between five and ten times as it grows into an adult. In most types of insect there are no more molts after this. The adult insect is called an **imago**.

The nymphs of some kinds of insects, such as dragonflies and damselflies, spend their lives in water before they turn into adults. Nymphs that live in water are called **naiads**. These do look slightly different from the adults because they live in water. The adults live on land and in the air.

▼ This is a mayfly nymph in a stream. As an adult it will have wings, but it will lose its feathery gills, which are on its abdomen and allow it to breathe under water.

▲ A young adult desert locust with its wings fully developed.

A desert locust nymph. It does not have adult wings yet, just small wing buds.

EGG-LAYING

Insects usually lay their eggs near a food supply for the young insects that will hatch out. The caterpillars that hatch from moth and butterfly eggs will usually only eat one type of plant. So the eggs must be laid on that kind of plant.

Flies often lay their eggs on rotting meat. The maggots will eat this when they hatch. One type of fly lays her eggs in front of a worker ant. The ant then picks the eggs up and carries them to the ants' nest, where they can hatch safely.

Many types of insect have a long tube called an **ovipositor** that lets them place their eggs where they want them.

Some insects take great care of their eggs. Female cockroaches often carry their eggs around with them, and female earwigs will stand guard over their eggs.

While it is inside the egg the growing young insect feeds on liquid yolk. When it is ready to hatch the insect must get out of the egg. Some types of insect have sharp spines that they use to cut through the tough eggshell. Others will swell up until they are too big for the egg and simply burst out. For many young insects their eggshell will be their very first meal.

All these maggots (top) probably ▲ hatched from one lot of eggs.

A shield bug keeps a close watch on her eggs. You can also see young shield bugs in the picture. ▶

A caterpillar hatches
from its egg. ▶

WALKING AND JUMPING

Have you ever wondered what it would be like to walk with six legs? How would you move them? Insects move their legs three at a time. The middle leg on one side moves at the same time as the first and last legs on the other side. The insect always has three legs on the ground at any time so it won't fall over.

An insect's legs are covered with a hard cuticle just like the rest of its body. The legs aren't just simple tubes. If they were the insect couldn't bend them and wouldn't be able to walk! Each leg has a number of different parts and can move where the parts join. All animals with exoskeletons, such as spiders, crabs and lobsters, have legs like this.

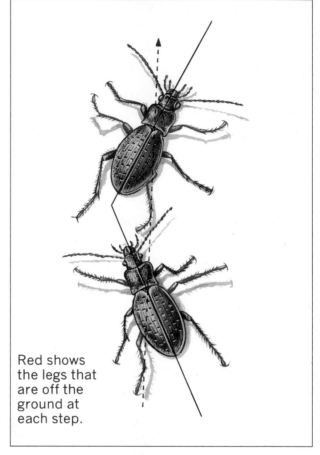

Red shows the legs that are off the ground at each step.

▲ Because insects always have one more leg pushing on one side than the other they tend to walk in a slight zigzag.

◄ You can see the claws on this beetle's legs that help it hold on to rough surfaces.

The legs of many insects have claws on the end that the insect uses to hold on to the surface it is walking on. Flies have sticky pads that allow them to climb up smooth surfaces such as glass and to hold on upside down on ceilings.

Many kinds of insect can jump as well as walk. The back legs of insects such as grasshoppers are much bigger than their other legs. They have powerful muscles inside. They jump in the same way you do, by bending their legs as far as they will go and then pushing up into the air.

Caterpillars can have as many as twenty-four legs. They use them to hold on to the surface they are walking on but not to pull themselves forward. They actually move by stretching their bodies forward a bit at a time. The legs are pulled in out of the way while that bit of the body is moving.

▲ As with all adult insects, a grasshopper's legs are jointed. It uses its long back legs to jump.

▼ Caterpillars use their legs to hold on with rather than for walking.

WINGS AND FLYING

Most types of insect can fly. Insects' wings are not made of feathers like birds' wings are. Each wing is, in fact, two very thin sheets of the cuticle that surrounds the insect's body. They are joined to the body by a hinge so they can move.

Many insects have two pairs of wings. Some, such as flies, gnats and mosquitoes, have only one pair. Instead of a second pair of wings they have a pair of little knobs called **halteres**. These beat at the same speed as the wings and help to keep the insect steady as it flies.

▲ Monarch butterflies make long journeys to and from their winter feeding grounds. Here, they pause for a drink.

You can see this ▲ cranefly's halteres just in front of its last pair of legs. They help it to fly steadily.

▲ A ladybird holds out its protective front wings when it flies. This gives it extra lift.

The front wings of beetles are thick and horny. When the beetle is on the ground they are used to protect the other pair of wings that are used for flying.

An insect's wings beat up and down very quickly. This creates a stream of air that pushes the insect up and forward. Muscles in the insect's thorax move the wings.

Some insects are very agile fliers. They can change direction very rapidly or hover in one spot. Some can even fly backward. Certain types of moth and horsefly can reach speeds of almost 30 miles per hour. Many insects fly for long distances. Some types of butterfly travel hundreds of miles to reach warm places to spend the winter.

►
This bumblebee's front and back pairs of wings are joined together by tiny hooks.

SEEING AND HEARING

Many types of insect have very big eyes. The eyes of flies and dragonflies seem to take up most of their heads. The bulging eyes of an insect are made up of thousands of tiny **lenses**, all packed closely together. These are called **compound** eyes. We don't know how the world looks through compound eyes – you'd have to be an insect to know that. Dragonflies' large eyes let them see well enough to catch mosquitoes flying at dusk.

As well as their compound eyes, insects also have simple eyes called **ocelli**. These are sensitive to changes in brightness.

The huge compound eyes of a horsefly. ▲

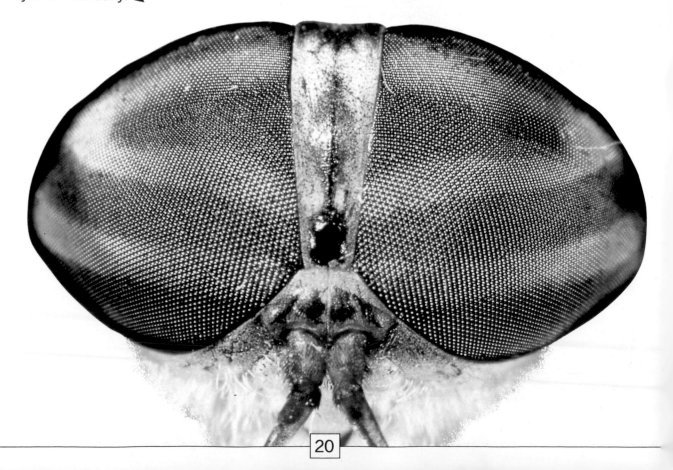

Larvae have only ocelli. They can just see well enough to find things to climb. This is what a caterpillar is looking for when it moves its head from side to side.

No insects have ears like we have, but most kinds can still hear sounds. Sounds are really just vibrations in the air. Most insects have hairs on their bodies that can pick up these vibrations just as well as ears do. In this way the insect can detect the sounds. Male mosquitoes use their antennae to pick up the vibrations made by the wingbeats of female mosquitoes.

Insects such as crickets make sounds by rubbing their back legs together. They do this to attract a **mate**. Bits of skin on their front legs vibrate in just the same way as the **eardrums** inside your ears do. This allows them to hear the sounds.

▶ A ten-spot dragonfly about to take off on a twilight hunt.

◀ This lubber grasshopper makes a sound by drawing little pegs on its hind legs across the surface of its front wing. Its ear is on its thorax. You can see it just under the wing. The small picture below gives you a closer look at the ear.

TASTING AND SMELLING

Most insects are more sensitive to taste and smell than to sound and light. The world must be a very different place to them than it is to us.

All insects have a pair of antennae on their heads. These antennae are also called feelers, and this is what many insects use them for. Some types of beetle have very long antennae to feel with. Ants will generally feel each other with their antennae when they meet. They are not just feeling, though. They are also tasting and smelling each other. Many insects use their antennae to smell and taste food.

Male moths use their antennae to smell out female moths. They are very sensitive, and some can detect the scents of a female several miles away.

Insects can also taste using their mouths and legs. They have sensitive hairs there that tell the insect about what it is tasting. Some types of butterfly have legs that are more than 200 times better at tasting sugar than a human's tongue is.

Hairs on an insect's body also give it information about what is touching it. Many beetles hide away under tree bark. Their sensitive hairs let them know when they are completely covered.

The feathery ▲ antennae of this silk moth are very sensitive to the scent of a female silk moth.

Did you know?

A fly can taste a drop of sugar with the tip of just one hair on the end of its leg.

22

▲ Ants recognize members of their
own nest by touching with
their antennae.

◀ The long antennae
of this elder borer
beetle are very good
at tasting and
smelling.

INSECT FEEDING

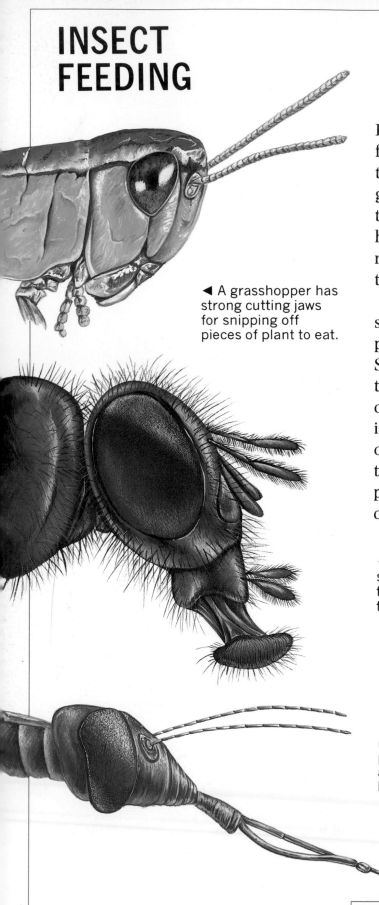

◀ A grasshopper has strong cutting jaws for snipping off pieces of plant to eat.

Insects have many different ways of feeding, depending on the type of food they eat. Some kinds of insect, such as grasshoppers and beetles, have mouths that can bite and chew. Their mouths have strong, toothed plates, called mandibles, that bite and tear the plants they eat.

Other insects use their mouths for sucking. The mouths of flies have soft parts like sponges that soak up liquids. Some insects have a **proboscis**, a long, tonguelike mouth part that sucks, pierces or laps up food. The mosquito's proboscis is like a hollow needle. It pierces the skin of animals so the mosquito can suck up their blood. Other insects have tubelike proboscises that stick into plants to suck out the sap.

◀ A fly has a sort of soft pad that it uses to soften its food and then suck it up.

◀ A mosquito uses its needlelike mouth to pierce the skin of an animal for a meal of blood.

Butterflies and moths feed on the sugary **nectar** inside flowers. They have long proboscises through which they can suck from deep in the flower, a bit like drinking through a straw. The proboscis is carried coiled up while the insect is flying.

Bees have hairy proboscises that can suck and chew. They use them to get **pollen** and nectar from inside flowers. They lap up the nectar rather than sucking it. Many types of bee carry pollen back to their nests to feed their larvae. Their back legs have stiff hairs on them that form little baskets to carry the pollen in. Other bees carry pollen in the hairs on their bellies.

Butterflies and ◀ moths have long tongues to reach the nectar deep inside flowers.

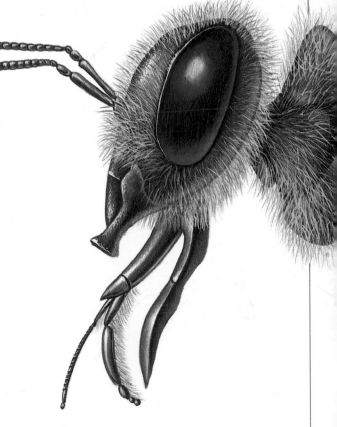

As well as feeding on liquid nectar, bees eat pollen grains from flowers. ▶

Did you know?

Most insects eat plants, but earwigs will nibble household scraps and bars of soap. Cockroaches will even eat old boots.

INSECT DEFENSES

Insects are food for many different animals—including other insects! So they have a variety of ways of avoiding being eaten. The most obvious way for many insects is to fly away. Some insects, such as cockroaches, don't fly but run very quickly from the slightest sign of danger. Others—crickets and fleas, for instance—will suddenly jump away.

Some insects taste very bad to anything that tries to eat them. Often bad-tasting insects are brightly colored to warn other animals not to eat them. Others smell terrible if touched. Some types of beetle defend themselves in this way. They also have hard outer casings for protection.

The black and yellow stripes of this wasp beetle might make a bird think it had a sting like a real wasp.

Wasps and bees have stings that they can use to attack anything that threatens their nests. Only the females have stings. Hoverflies and wasp beetles have black and yellow stripes, just like wasps, but no sting. Other animals don't realize this, however, and leave them alone. Many ants have stings, too. Some types of ant don't have stings but can squirt acid up to 10 inches away. Some moth larvae can squirt acid as well.

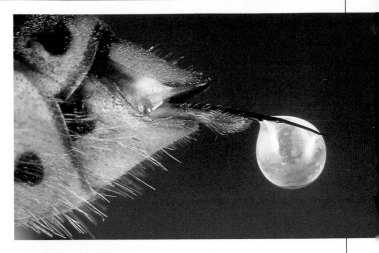

▲ A close-up view of a drop of poison on a hornet's sting.

◀ The strong colors of this moth larva warn birds that it will be unpleasant to eat.

▼ This stick insect is doubly protected – firstly, by its leafy color and shape; secondly, by its curling tail, which makes it look like a stinging scorpion.

One of the best ways of avoiding being attacked is by not being seen. Many insects are very well **camouflaged**. Their patterns and colors blend so well into the background that they become very difficult to see. Other types of insect hide themselves by looking like something else. Some insects look so much like leaves that sometimes they get bitten by leaf-eating animals. Some caterpillars look almost exactly like bird droppings!

INSECTS
EVERYWHERE

A stag beetle. ►
Beetles are the most
successful type of
insect. They come in
a huge variety of
shapes and sizes.

There are probably more different types of
insect than there are different types of all
the other animals put together. More than
one million kinds of insect have been
named, and several thousand more are
added every year. There are more than
350,000 known kinds of beetle alone. No one
knows how many insects there might be.

Insects live just about everywhere.
Some types can be found in the cold polar
regions, where they keep warm by living
in the fur and feathers of mammals and
birds. Countless numbers live in the
jungles of the world. A few types live on
the sea. Because young insects, the larvae
and nymphs, are different from the adults,
they can live in different places.

Although insects come in a huge variety of shapes and forms, they all have certain things in common. Every insect, at some point in its life, has six legs, and most usually have two pairs of wings. All adult insects have a pair of antennae and most have a pair of compound eyes. Their bodies are divided into three parts.

It is impossible to imagine life without insects. There have been insects in the world for many millions of years. They form a vital part of the living world, enabling the survival of many other animals and plants.

GLOSSARY

Abdomen: The end part of an insect's body.

Adult: An insect or other animal that is fully grown.

Antennae: A pair of feelers on an insect's head that the insect uses to touch, smell and taste with. A single one of these is called an antenna.

Arteries: Arteries and veins are the names given to the tubes that carry blood around the body in animals such as birds and mammals. Insects do not have arteries and veins.

Camouflage: Colors or patterns on something that help to hide it by blending in with its background.

Chitin: The tough material that makes up an insect's outer coat, or *cuticle.*

Cocoon: A covering that a *larva* makes to protect itself when it becomes a *pupa.*

Compound: The term used to describe the large eyes of animals such as insects, shrimps, crabs and lobsters. They are made up of many tiny *lenses.* Human eyes have only one lens.

Cuticle: The tough outside part of an insect, made of *chitin.* The cuticle forms the insect's *exoskeleton.*

Digestive system: The parts inside an animal's body that break down its food to provide the energy and chemical substances the animal needs to live.

Eardrum: The part of an ear that vibrates in response to sound waves. The vibrations are then passed on to the ear bones and from there to the inner ear and then to the brain.

Exoskeleton: A tough, stiff, outer covering for the bodies of some types of animal, such as insects, spiders and crabs. It protects and supports the body.

Ganglia: Parts of an insect's *nervous system* that control different parts of its body. A single one of these is called a ganglion.

Gizzard: A tough, muscular part of an insect's *digestive system* that grinds food into small pieces. Many types of bird have gizzards.

Halteres: Two-winged flies have these where other insects would have a second pair of wings. They help the insect to fly steadily.

Head: For insects, the head is the first part of its three-sectioned body. An insect's mouth parts, eyes and *antennae* are found on its head.

Imago: A fully grown *adult* insect.

Larva: The young of an insect (and some other animals) after it hatches from the egg; more than one are called larvae. It does not look like the adult it will become later. Caterpillars are butterfly larvae; tadpoles are frog larvae.

Lens: The part of the eye that directs light into the eye to form a sharp picture. The *compound* eyes of insects have many tiny lenses.

Mate: One of a pair of animals, one male and the other female, who together will produce young.

Metamorphosis: The change from a *larva* to an *adult* insect that takes place in a *pupa*.

Naiad: A name sometimes given to a young insect, or *nymph*, that lives in water.

Nectar: The sweet, sugary substance produced by some flowers to attract animals. When an animal eats the nectar, *pollen* in the flower sticks to its body. The animal then leaves this pollen in other flowers it visits. This enables the flowers to produce their seeds.

Nervous system: The part of an animal's body, including its brain, that sends messages from one part of the body to another and controls what the animal does.

Nymph: The young of some types of insect. They look very much like the *adults* except that they have no wings. They become adults without forming a *pupa* like a *larva* does. A nymph that lives in water is often called a *naiad*.

Ocelli: Simple eyes that insects and some other animals have. They can only detect differences in brightness. A single one of these is called an ocellus.

Ovipositor: The part of a female insect's *abdomen* through which she lays her eggs.

Pollen: Tiny orange or yellow grains produced by the male parts of flowering and cone-bearing plants.

Proboscis: The long mouth parts of some insects that are used to reach food.

Pupa: The stage between *larva* and *adult* when *metamorphosis* takes place. During this time the insect does not feed.

Skeleton: The framework of bones inside the bodies of animals such as birds, reptiles and mammals. It supports the body and protects the parts inside.

Spiracles: The openings of the *trachea* on the outside of an insect's body. Air enters through the spiracles.

Thorax: The middle section of an insect's body to which the wings and legs are attached.

Trachea: Tiny tubes inside an insect's body that take air into the body from the *spiracles*.

Veins: See *Arteries*.

INDEX

Abdomen, 6, 7, 30
Antennae, 6, 22, 23, 29, 30
Ants, 5, 14, 22, 23, 27
Aphids, 10, 11
Arteries, 8, 30

Bees, 10, 25, 27
  bumblebees, 19
Beetles, 5, 7, 11, 16, 19, 22,
  26, 29
  elder borer, 23
  green tiger, 4
  stag, 28-29
  wasp, 26, 27
Birds, 8, 18, 28, 30, 31
Blood, 8, 9, 24, 30
Brain, 8, 9, 30, 31
Butterflies, 5, 10, 14, 19, 22,
  24, 30
  monarch, 18
  peacock, 2, 5

Camouflage, 27, 30
Caterpillars, 2, 3, 5, 9, 10, 14,
  15, 17, 21, 30
Centipedes, 7
Chitin, 7, 30
Cockroaches, 14, 25, 26
Cocoon, 11, 30
Crabs, 16, 31
Cranefly, 18
Crickets, 21, 26
Cuticle, 7, 16, 18, 30

Damselflies, 12
Desert locust, 13
Digestive system, 8, 9, 30
Dragonflies, 12, 20
  ten-spot, 20-21

Eardrums, 21, 30
Ears, 21, 30
Earwigs, 12, 14, 25
Eggs, 10, 12, 14, 31
  -laying, 14
  yolk, 14
Exoskeleton, 7, 16, 30
Eyes, 6, 20, 21
  compound (large), 6, 20, 29,
    30
  ocelli (small), 6, 20, 21, 31

Flies, 5, 10, 14, 17, 18, 20, 22,
  24, 31
  blowfly, 4
  horsefly, 19, 20
Flying, 9, 19-20

Ganglion (*pl.* ganglia), 8, 9, 30
Gnats, 18
Gizzard, 8, 30
Grasshoppers, 12, 17, 24
  lubber, 21
Grubs, 10, 11

Hairs, 21, 22, 25
Halteres, 18, 30
Head, 6, 9, 30
Hornets, 11, 27
Humans, 8, 9, 21, 22, 31

Imago, 12, 13, 30
Insects, 1-31
  adult, 6, 10, 11, 30. *See also*
    Imago
  defenses, 26-27
  external body structure, 6-7,
    29
  feeding, 24-25
  internal body structure, 8-9
  life cycle, 10-15

Jaws, 7
Jumping, 17

Ladybirds, 10, 11, 19
Larva (*pl.* larvae), 10, 11, 21,
  25, 27, 28, 30
Legs, 6, 7, 16, 17, 22, 25, 29, 31
Lenses, 20, 31
Lobsters, 7, 16, 31

Maggots, 10, 14
Mammals, 28, 30, 31
Mate, 21, 31
Mayfly, 12
Metamorphosis, 11, 30
Molting, 12
Mosquitoes, 18, 20, 21, 24
Moths, 10, 14, 19, 22, 25, 27
  death's-head, 2
  silk, 22
  tiger, 1, 2

Mouth parts, 6, 22, 24, 25,
  30, 31

Naiads, 12, 31
Nectar, 2, 25, 31
Nervous sytem, 9, 31
Nests, 10, 11, 14, 23, 25, 27
Nymphs, 12, 13, 28, 31

Ovipositor, 14, 31

Pollen, 25, 31
Proboscis, 24, 25, 31
Pupa, 11, 31

Shield bugs, 7, 14
Skeleton, 7, 31
Smelling, 22-23
Spiders, 5, 6, 7, 16
Spiracles, 7, 8, 9, 31
Stick insects, 27
Sugar, 22

Tasting, 22-23
Thorax, 6, 7, 9, 19, 31
Thrips, 5
Trachea, 8, 9, 31

Veins, 8, 30, 31

Wasps, 11, 27
Walking, 9, 14, 16-17
Wings, 6, 12, 13, 19-20, 29, 31

J 595.7/SNE
SNEDDEN, ROBERT.
WHAT IS AN INSECT? /
1ST U.S. ED.
1993, c1992. 32883262

CC   DEC   1993

SCARBOROUGH PUBLIC LIBRARY

3 9017 02603 9981

Q July 01

L

THE
SCARBOROUGH
PUBLIC LIBRARY
BOARD